The Golden Girls

A Guided Journal

RP STUDIO

PHILADELPHIA

RP Studio™
Hachette Book Group
1290 Avenue of the Americas, New York, NY 10104
www.runningpress.com
@Running_Press

Printed in China

First Edition: June 2020

Published by RP Studio, an imprint of Perseus Books, LLC, a subsidiary of Hachette Book Group, Inc. The RP Studio name and logo is a trademark of the Hachette Book Group.

The publisher is not responsible for websites (or their content) that are not owned by the publisher.

Design by Joshua McDonnell.
Text by Christine Kopaczewski.

ISBN: 978-0-7624-7125-6

1010

10 9 8 7 6 5 4 3 2 1

Write a letter to your younger self here.
What do you need to say?

Whether it's literary masterpieces, a laundry list
of suitors, or a convoluted St. Olaf story,
list ten things that make you smile.

_____
_____
_____
_____
_____
_____
_____
_____
_____
_____
_____
_____
_____
_____
_____
_____
_____
_____
_____
_____

Dorothy and Blanche have had their quibbles, but at the end of the day they're thick as thieves. Describe one of your closest friends and what they mean to you.

What is your favorite way to spend the day?

_____

_____

_____

_____

_____

_____

_____

_____

_____

_____

_____

_____

_____

_____

_____

_____

What are some of your wishes and hopes for the future?

Blanche forces Rose to learn ballroom dancing, only to get miffed when Rose outshines her on the dancefloor. What's something you want to learn but have been too afraid to try?

....
....
....
....
....
....
....
....
....
....
....
....
....
....
....
....
....
....
....
....
....
....
....
....
....

What are some of the biggest moments of your
life so far? How have they changed you?

Blanche and Rose met at the community bulletin board in the grocery store. What's the story behind meeting your best friend?

Blanche often describes herself as devastatingly beautiful. What two words would you use to describe yourself and why?

Picture it: Sicily. If you could paint a picture of
your favorite memory, what would it look like?

When old friends of Sophia and Salvadore—
the Boscos—visit Brooklyn, Dorothy is convinced
Sophia isn't her biological mother. Did you ever think
you were switched at birth? Why or why not?

Rose tends to have a different slant on life than
the rest of the girls. What do you believe in
that most don't? Why?

_____
_____
_____
_____
_____
_____
_____
_____
_____
_____
_____
_____
_____
_____
_____
_____
_____
_____
_____
_____
_____
_____

After winning $10,000 on a lottery ticket, the girls dream up big ways to spend the money, before generously deciding to donate it to a local homeless shelter. If you won the lottery tomorrow, what would you do with the money?

_____

_____

_____

_____

_____

_____

_____

_____

_____

_____

_____

_____

_____

_____

_____

_____

_____

_____

_____

Sophia's known for her sauce, the other three for their love of cheesecake. Pick one food that defines you and explain why.

Blanche tells Dorothy not all of her dreams are sexual—sometimes she dreams about food. What is the craziest dream you've had and what do you think it means?

Rose and Dorothy uprooted their lives to move to Miami and try something new. If you were to leave your home today, where would you go next?

Rose loves all things St. Olaf.

What's your favorite thing about your hometown?

Dorothy loves to read books that leave her with a new perspective on life. Name a book that changed the way you see the world and write about why it altered your perspective.

....
....
....
....
....
....
....
....
....
....
....
....
....
....
....
....
....
....
....
....
....
....
....
....
....
....

Who can forget about the time the girls decided to buy and breed minks?! What's the weirdest thing you've ever done?

What qualities make someone a good friend?

Blanche is known for being sexy; Sophia is sarcastic; Dorothy is witty; and Rose is sweet. What is your most defining characteristic?

Rose admits to being somewhat of a rebel
(she enjoys eating raw cookie dough, running through
sprinklers without a bathing cap, and indulging
in more than one eggnog during the holidays).
Have you ever had a rebellious streak?

Stanley and Dorothy's cat and mouse game is a classic trope on exes. Do you have a love/hate relationship with someone?

....
....
....
....
....
....
....
....
....
....
....
....
....
....
....
....
....
....
....
....
....
....
....
....
....
....
....
....

Rose, Blanche, and Sophia coped with the void created when their husbands passed away. Do you have a void in your life? What's causing it?

....
....
....
....
....
....
....
....
....
....
....
....
....
....
....
....
....
....
....
....
....
....
....
....
....
....
....

Create your own perfect flavor of cheesecake.

Dorothy is passionate about addressing what she sees as the country's lackluster education system. What issues are you passionate about and why?

Blanche loves to gush about her first time(s).
What was your most memorable rite of passage?

. . . .
. . . .
. . . .
. . . .
. . . .
. . . .
. . . .
. . . .
. . . .
. . . .
. . . .
. . . .
. . . .
. . . .
. . . .
. . . .
. . . .
. . . .
. . . .
. . . .
. . . .

The Petrillo family sauce is an art form carried
down by generations of Sicilian women.
Does your family have a signature recipe?
Why is it so important to you?

Dorothy and Sophia have their ups and downs, but at the end of the day they share an unbreakable bond. How is your relationship with your parents? Would you ship them off to Shady Pines or let them stay with you?

Blanche decided her own life story
was worthy of a book. Is yours?
Write the first chapter.

_____

_____

_____

_____

_____

_____

_____

_____

_____

_____

_____

_____

_____

_____

_____

_____

_____

_____

_____

_____

Between Stanley, the philandering salesman, Miles, the man of mystery, and a roster of Rusty Anchor regulars, the girls have had some pretty memorable exes. Who is your most memorable ex? Why?

The lanai is the centerpiece to the girls' home. Where's your favorite place to unwind and spend time? Why?

_____

_____

_____

_____

_____

_____

_____

_____

_____

_____

_____

_____

_____

_____

_____

_____

_____

_____

_____

Rose loves classic St. Olaf games. What's your favorite childhood game? Why do you love it?

. . . .
. . . .
. . . .
. . . .
. . . .
. . . .
. . . .
. . . .
. . . .
. . . .
. . . .
. . . .
. . . .
. . . .
. . . .
. . . .
. . . .
. . . .

What would you most like to be remembered for?

Go on and blow your own vertubenflugen—
what have you accomplished in your lifetime
that you are most proud of?

....
....
....
....
....
....
....
....
....
....
....
....
....
....
....
....
....
....
....
....
....
....
....
....
....
....
....
....
....

Each of the girls is involved in philanthropic efforts, whether it's delivering meals to the elderly or raising funds to save the wetlands. If you were going to start a charity, what would it be and who or what would it benefit?

What things mean the most to you at this point in your life?

_____

_____

_____

_____

_____

_____

_____

_____

_____

_____

_____

_____

_____

_____

_____

_____

_____

_____

Rose gave a spirited acceptance speech for the Volunteer of the Year award she *didn't* win. Write an acceptance speech for an award you haven't received yet but hope to one day.

Dorothy, Rose, Blanche, or Sophia—
which of the girls do you personally
relate to the most? Why?

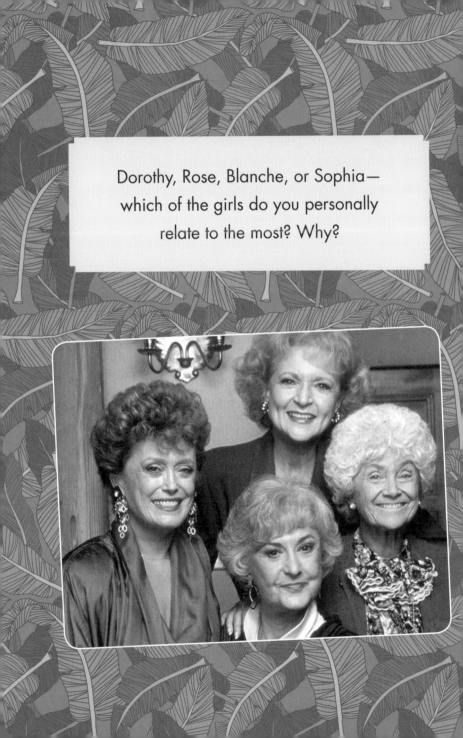

What do you wish others knew about you?

Rose vividly remembers making her own Christmas present (shoes she'd carved out of coal . . . don't ask how), and how that moment taught her to be resourceful. What childhood memory of yours stands out as a defining moment?

After hearing of a planned demolition, Blanche couldn't bear the thought of losing her grammy's house. What place makes you sentimental? What happened there?

Sophia set sail for America on her own after annulling her first marriage—much to her family's disapproval. Name a time when you took a chance and followed your heart even when others disagreed.

Write out the inside of a birthday card to your best friend.

Decades after being stood up on her prom night,
Dorothy reconnected with her first crush, John,
only to find him dreamier than ever.
Who was your very first crush?
Would you still like those qualities in a partner today?

When Rose made her news anchor debut, she went viral (unfortunately for all the wrong reasons). If you were to star in a viral video, what would be going on and what would you be doing?

Do you have any regrets? How do you handle them?

What's the most interesting or unique
quality about your generation?
Is that a good thing or a bad thing?

Sophia often uses her sarcasm and tough love as a way of teaching the girls important life lessons. What's your love language with friends and family? How do you show it?

Growing up, Rose had a pet pig, Mr. Snuffles.
He was her best friend until he ran away.
If you could communicate with animals,
what species would you talk to and why?

Dorothy can rock a set of shoulder pads like no other. What item of clothing or accessory best defines your personal style?

Blanche, Rose, Dorothy, and Sophia all have beef with their siblings. Do you have any sibling rivalry? What causes it?

....
....
....
....
....
....
....
....
....
....
....
....
....
....
....
....
....
....
....
....
....
....
....
....
....
....
....
....

Sophia once told Dorothy: "Jealousy is an ugly thing, and so are you in anything backless." Ouch! What's the honest bit of truth you've been given by a loved one?

What makes you happiest?

During a near death experience, Sophia headed into the light and saw her beloved Salvadore again. Do you believe in an afterlife?

After big life moments, the girls gather around the table and gush over cheesecake. What's your favorite friendship ritual?

If you could tell your future self three things,
what would they be?